Cat with Piano Tuna
and Other Feline Nonsense

Drawings and Verses
by Simon Drew

bureaucat

ANTIQUE COLLECTORS' CLUB,

to Caroline
and the Donaldsons' cats

©1990 Simon Drew
World copyright reserved
First published 1990
Reprinted October 1990

ISBN 1 85149 138 4

British Library Cataloguing in
Publication Data
Drew, Simon
  Cat with piano tuna and other
  feline nonsense.
  1. Graphic arts. Special subjects:
  Cats 2. Poetry. Special subjects:
  Cats — Anthologies
  I. Title
  760 . 04432

Published and printed in England by the Antique Collectors' Club Ltd.,
Woodbridge, Suffolk.

hear no fish, see no fish, speak no fish

I have such a passion for hedges
I made for this cat with a bee-line.
I offered to give it
a sample of privet
and now it appears
it's grown it for years.
It cut silhouettes
of its parents and pets
and created a feline-shaped treeline.

A character wearing a cycle
was wandering past me by chance:
    to my way of thinking
    he must have been drinking.
I asked him the reason:
he said, "It's the season
to enter the next Tour de France."

cat with open toad sandal

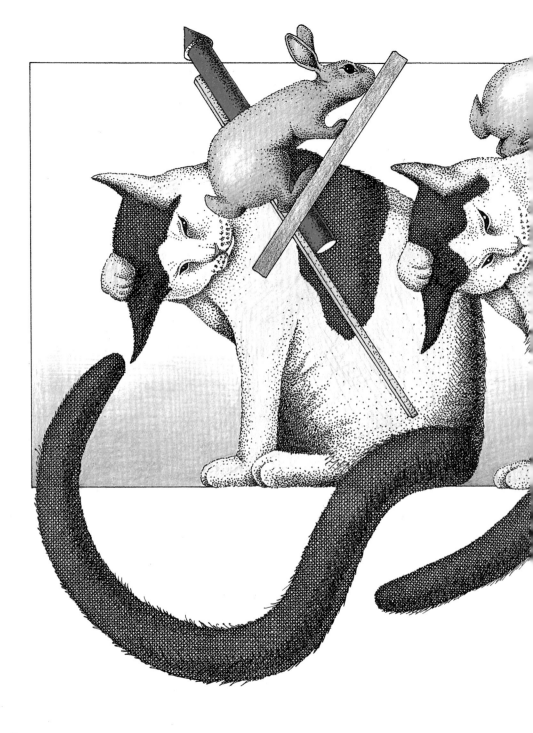

A cat with a passion for jelly
would carry one shaped like a rabbit
but one night a rocket
it kept in its pocket
was lit by some matches
(a cat always scratches)
and halted its lunatic habit.

From gelatine to gelignite
that cat discovered space that night.

drew

Last year on the first of November
a cat in our town wore a trifle
        to honour his cousin
        who'd eaten a dozen
        to win a small wager
        he'd had with a major.
        (The cousin's endeavour
        was finished forever
by marksmen who passed with a rifle.)

A cat that lived mainly with mallards
developed a liking for pears,
  and soon became fatter
  by eating the latter
and so needed reinforced chairs.

So he thought he would try a new diet,
disheartened by everyone's stares.
  He's now saturated
  by grapes dehydrated
and calls them his currant affairs.

13

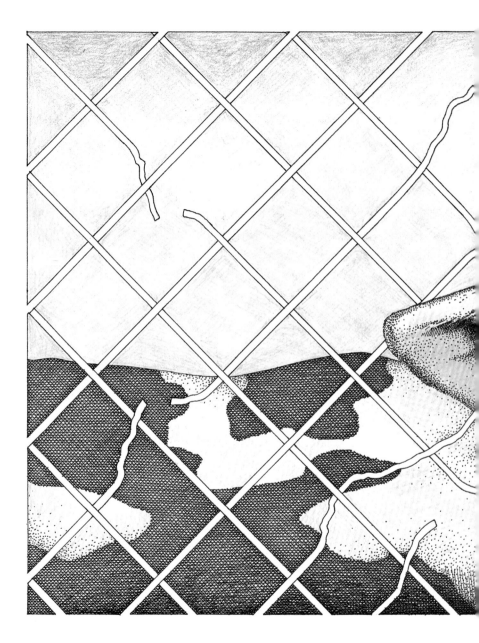

cat with sacred cow

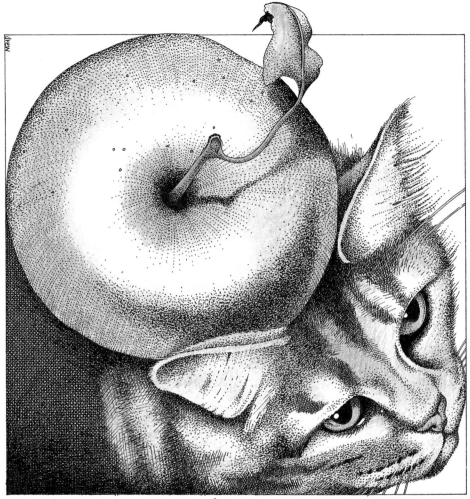

A sinister cat with an apple
would often expound his new theories
on how to determine
the worst sort of vermin
and how you should never
pretend to be clever
and how beneficial a beer is.

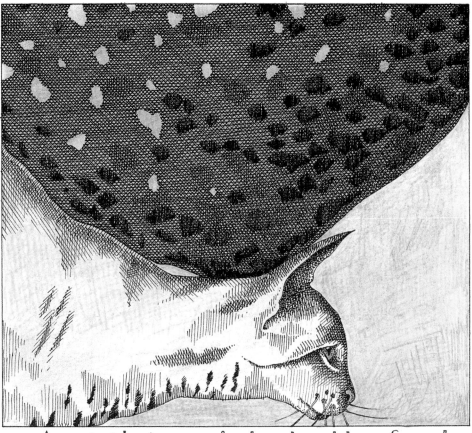

A cat that carried a boulder of rock
for the best part of twenty one years
    said: "Once I had trouble
    while bearing this rubble;
    round Switzerland's borders,
    by strict doctor's orders,
    I'd walked and perspired
    and a rest was required.
    But just as I'd halted
    my rock was assaulted
by short-sighted Swiss mountaineers.

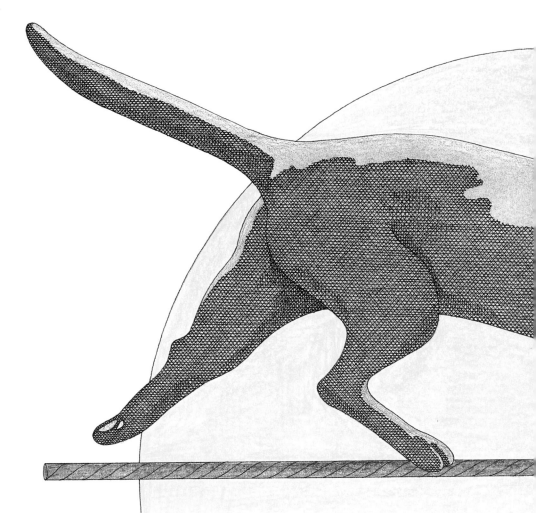

Political cats on a tightrope
are almost as rare as a ruby.
The reason appears......

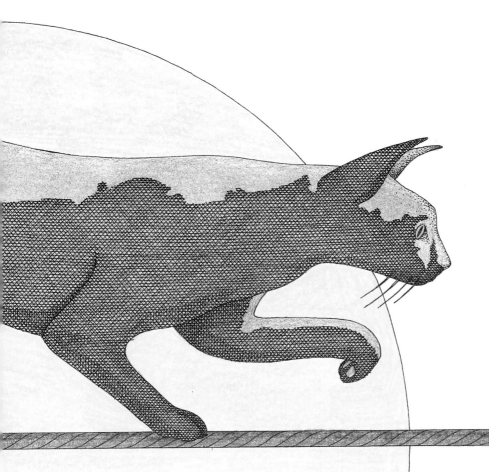

they all have great fears
of a swing to the right
on the next voting night,
or a swing to the left
(which would leave them bereft)
and they're frightened of heights.
Wouldn't you be?

19

The only cat left in our village
can balance four eggs on its paws.
This talented action
has caused a reaction . . . . .

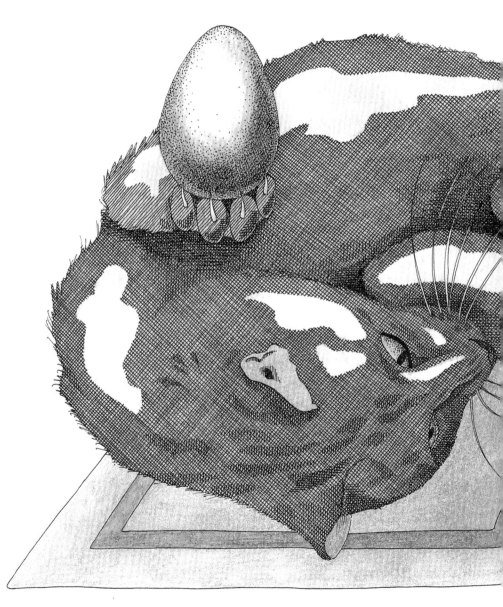

amongst all the foxes
who come with egg boxes
and tickle each trotter
to make the eggs totter
to catch them unscathed in their jaws.

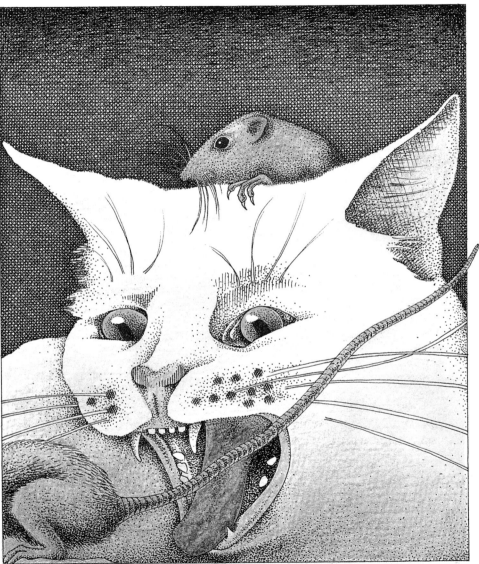

There's a cat in the suburbs of Moscow
with mice who will come when they're beckoned.
The methods of killing
are what he finds thrilling:
his friends call him Stalin the Second.

A french philosophical feline
supported a sink full of jam.
This strange aberration
had one explanation:
"I sink and so therefore I am."

A cat in this tale runs a circus
and finds a princess that he marries.
On the flying trapeze
with the maximum ease
they fly through the air
with the minimum care.
So what is the factor
that seems to attract her?
It must be the magnet he carries.

cat with pig iron and fish tank

A cat with a circular halo
could never resist a lost cause –
   a preoccupation
   with saving the nation
   from drinkers and sinners
   and microwave dinners
and humans that crawl on all-fours.

The sun is setting and nobody cares;
the evening has caught them all unawares.
The ploughman returns to his block of flats:
he's putting the pigeon among the cats.

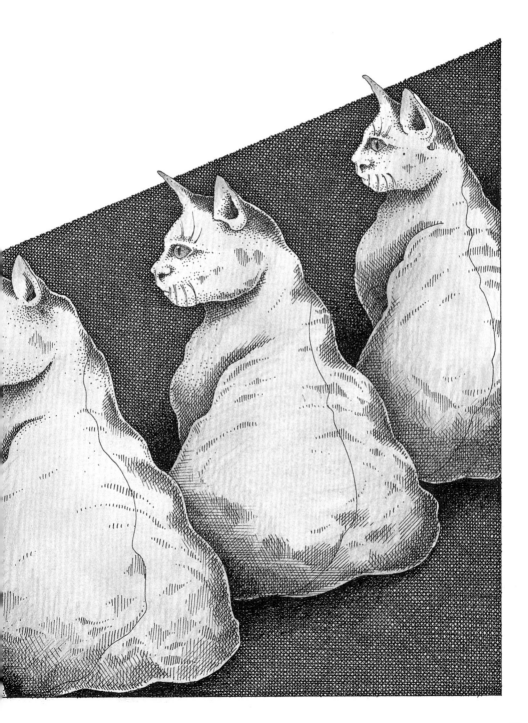

A cat with the colour of angels
was trying to balance a weasel
    with glasses of claret,
    while making a parrot
    in see-through apparel
    recite Lewis Carroll,
    to make the beast placid
    while feeding it acid
and plentiful helpings of diesel.

31

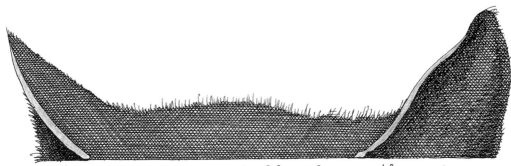

A cat that patrols Heathrow Airport
can juggle with duty-free wine,
but try as he might
with practice at night
he still finds it hard
to juggle with lard:
it's a technique he wants to refine.

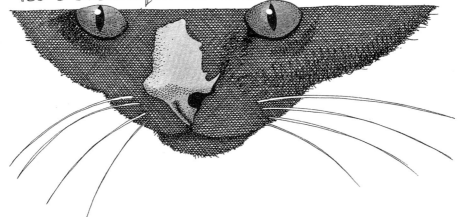

A cat balanced 98 paint tins
on various parts of its head
and as an encore
added twenty four more.
Result: they came down
and painted the town
a surprisingly nice shade of red.

On a journey through Rome I discovered
a cat that had claimed to be Caesar.
    He sported an eagle
    to make himself regal
    and wreaths made of laurel
    and anything floral.
    Forgetting its meaning
    this pile started leaning
suggesting his true home was Pisa.

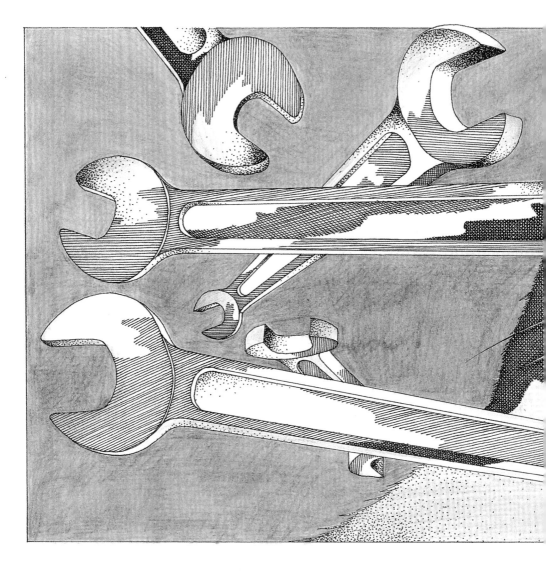

This cat performs tricks for the children
in a rather avuncular manner:
    with hardly a jolt
    he swallows a bolt
    then adds to his guts
    some stainless steel nuts
and tightens them up with a spanner. drew

It was difficult to guess just what they were:
they had bodies clothed in coats of silken fur.
They had crossed my headlight beam without a sound
and it seemed they made no contact with the ground.
They were stealthy as a bomb that won't explode:
they were cat-size in the middle of the road.

42

A cat carried glasses of fruit juice
despite never liking the taste,
    but while he was sleeping
    his friends entered creeping
    on dastardly missions,
    and little additions
    were made to the juices,
    with silent excuses.
(The drink in this picture is laced.)

cats will chew up beetles
they never pay their deep respects:
  they swipe at flies,
  they bite at fleas,
cats cannot stick stick insects.

Never trust a cat who's in disguise:
Never trust a parrot telling lies.
While you think his purrs are signs of joy
he's really asking: "Who's a pretty boy?"

A cat with a tap on each nostril
had never been noted for cunning.
The more that we saw it
we couldn't ignore it.
But soon it was clear:
he'd had an idea
for trying to stop his nose running.

How to make a cat pyramid:

One cat
Two cats
Three cats
Four
(Never fewer: never more)
Six on top and four on floor.
(Double this: produce a score).

A cat with a passion for Shakespeare
built a theatre from ear to ear:
    the proscenium arch
    was constructed of larch
    and with seating in rows
    on the tip of his nose
he's staging Much Do About Lear.

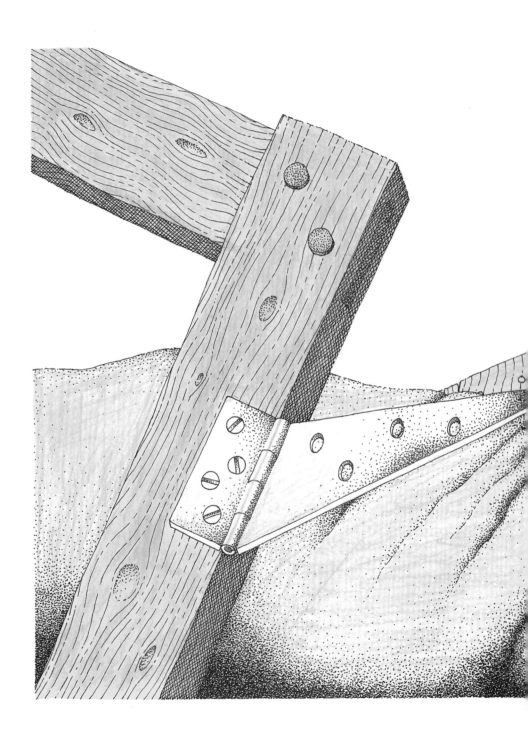